to a collector ---
from a butterfly---

Created by a woman known as Memere, remade by her
loving grandchildren Gretchen and Colleen Ehrhart

to our Memere; a wise,
generous, beautiful soul

TABLE OF CONTENTS

I

•

RESTLESS BUTTERFLY

restless butterfly
your beauty is so fragile
as you flit through life

perhaps the collector
is the only one who
really understands

escaped again–ah!
happily, alone, soundless,
my thoughts drift away.

why is it that the
weed i had neglected so
stole all the glory?

silent rings the night
summer flowers feel first chill,
kitten licks my toe.

fog spreads its cover
a bird pierces the grey veil
in soundless flight.

frost came through last night
and he didn't care what he took,
some buds never bloom.

a windy grey day
the sun now and then peeps through
all life seems restless.

the day is so long
the night is even longer
with full moon ablaze.

yellow goldenrod
strung together with bright webs
mistress of the field.

i hear you, old cat–
calling for love at twilight---
silently cry i.

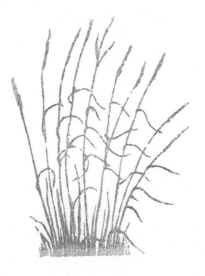

late blossom trembles
in fall's twilight, did you know
summer's soft caress?

dark days, dark thoughts, but
i know they will all pass, what
will be forever?

my heart heavy in
thought, suddenly, the full moon,
all seems magnified.

the chill in my heavy
heart, is surely a good match
for this grey day.

old tree seals itself
from the chill of winter winds
leaves blush, fade and die.

i picked a flower
to save her from the frosts kill–
alas, she died too.

my garden flowers
all bent and brown, you will not
know the chill to come.

i tried to cry tears
but wind came by and dried them—
my good mother earth.

father time moves on
mother earth with all she holds
bows low and changes.

captive beast pacing---
there is a beast deep inside
clawing at my soul.

the month of darkness
today presented a jewel
time to celebrate.

in the dark shadows
created by fall's twilight
i find time alone.

the colors are warm
but the day holds a great chill---
autumn's paradox.

great clouds of grey geese
darken the late autumn sky---
sounds drift to the earth.

autumn wind blew in
kindled an old flame of mine
and then passed on out.

patching up my house
against a nature that's so strong–
can i yet survive?

icy windy day
happily i slip-slide home
i see only jewels.

thawing out aches so---
i'm as foolish in winter
as any season.

your eyes caught my smile
a million words were unsaid
all in one moment.

it is not this chill
that has me trembling so---
but the awareness.

anticipation–
it turns my thoughts upside down
blinds me from the now.

II

·

I AM LIKE THE OAK

i am like the oak–
vulnerable to seasons
yet, i must stand tall.

this peaceful morning
belies the stormy white night
fickle friend of mine.

cat at my window
pink nose pressed against the glass–
powder puff warrior.

windy, white on white
the promised storm has arrived
silently, i watch.

breaking its silence,
snow tumbles from my roof top–
back to mother earth.

icicle shattered---
like my most delicate dreams---
just momentary.

fingers ache tonight
as i trudge through squeaking snow
but, my heart aches more.

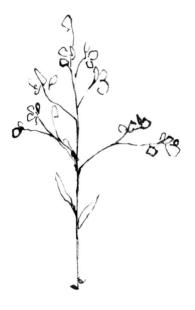

window filled with greens
how precious even the weed
against the white snow.

moist cool night moves on
a sensual touch–i–am
again in full bloom.

old cat crossed my mind
and woke again my most
pleasant memories.

i found him crying–
today--- and then he died–now
old cat–i cry too.

fragile remnants of
wild beauty, peeping through deep
snow–silent splendor.

giant puffs of white
the seasons first snow, dream i
of winter's glory.

heavy white silence
suddenly, happy noise, my
children are at play.

cat at my window
how fast you've checked your kingdom
wind blows at your fur.

countless grey days have
passed–but in truth, i have
noticed only a few.

my late summer plants
tenderly saved, wait patiently
for the springtime.

my garden companion
great whiskered smiles–stored now
in old memories.

old cat is gone now
hope you have sweet mice and
a lively mistress.

and now my little
garden, all frozen and brown
i still think of you.

i am a perennial–

just one sweet moment
is all we can ever have---
we bloom and we die.

i'm older now
and have had
a few sweet moments–

cool blue day's, bright blue
the hills were filled with chicory
all matched the days mood.

first warm day this year
a reunion with the sun
the celebration.

summer's evening sounds–
with gown and slippers i join
the happy concert.

white cloud of blossoms
silhouetted against black
soft rain and warm smiles.

plants reach to the sun
to find their strength and their growth
i have my source too.

white triad amid
the lush green–spark of light
to brighten my day.

endless fields of white
lace–like my love–a fragile
surface and deep roots.

a quiet moment---
one of those imperfect days,
have courage to dream.

my everyday spot
gaily dressed in summer's lace–
a place for day dreams.

summer's heat steams on–
cicada cries piercingly
and my thoughts simmer.

summer's eve daws near
the fog begins its creeping
all turns blue and grey.

seagull

white body bobbing
endless waves reflect the sun
little fisherman!

a blue-grey evening
staring in mirror-like water
first star–make a wish.

soundless evening lake
almost perfect mirror now
i sit and reflect.

in the summer's field
i sat to rest, and listen
to its hum---

to a wild flower

it is your nature
unafraid to fill your needs
dare i be like you?

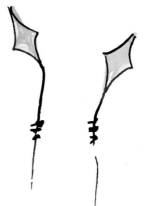

kites soared on the breeze
they appeared so free and grey---
but they too have strings.

cow slip–a swamp flower

i should be like you–
to know the source, and bravely
get my toes wet too.

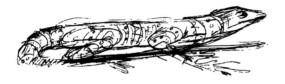

summer spreads fragile
lace, it fills the fields, a soft
bed for young dreamers.

a misty, morning
spider's web glistened brightly
thoughts turn to the fall.

great treasure hunting
standing in clear cool water
minnow moves slowly swiftly.

only a moment
can i ever dare to hold
perfection, gives way.

my unfulfilled dreams
of spring melt away to thoughts
of summers glory.

something in me is
dying–even as i watch
my spring garden grow.

clouds of white petals
dance against the dark blue sky–
rain smells sweet now.

i am tired now---
only the memory lasts
magic moment gone.

all is white and still
listen and let love enter
hear the song of peace.

silent frozen lake,
sounds crack in the frosty air
silver blades sparkle.

the wind whistles by–
and all seems adrift---
trees bend, so do i.

Hawaii

brown people, red earth
blue skies meeting a blue sea
wind and mountains wed.

bird, fly me away
i've been to paradise---
now home again, home.

bold plumeria
twigs and flowers do you bare
for maidens dark hair.

in a plane

the sky is mirrored---
blue and white, now white and blue–
i feel motionless.

caught in a car

the rain plays its tune–
and the wind whistles along---
captive, i listen.

approaching victory
and still, i cannot forget
the many defeats.

time, the great healer–
the most precious thing i have–
and yet so fleeting.

the fast is over–
and like the lush spring flowers
i am in full bloom.

cool misty morning
crickets and rooster mix song
the air smells of fall.

stalking the dark eve
my hungry thoughts heightened
by your faint outline.

in the dark silence
people move in private worlds---
sing a muted song.

time and a promise
carries me to the unknown bounds–
the sweet flight of life.

the end of the day
morning glory has given way
still, see the new bud?

I AM LIKE THE OAK

III

THEME AND VARIATION

theme and variation

dark strong huntress runs
chasing the old butterfly---
a game with no end

trees dressed in white gowns---
sway to winter's fickle time---
those that bend survive.

dark night and rains fell
i thought that i was dying---
the end never came.

**theme and variation
of the hunter**

> fall day, cool and bright---
> the huntress is out again
> chasing butterflies.

the hunter so brave
stalking the elusive prey---
poor old butterfly.

the nights are cold now
and the butterfly is gone---
hunter stalks alone.

ender theme and variation

the storms dark shadows
makes the rainbow more lovely
life's made of contrasts.

mistress of vision
by *Francis Thompson*

when to the new
eyes of thee
all things of immor-
tal power
near or far
hiddenly
to each other
linked are,
thou canst not
stir a flower
without troubling
of a star